The Green Route: Discovering the World Sustainably

Estelle-Maria Reed

Published by Estelle-Maria Reed, 2024.

While every precaution has been taken in the preparation of this book, the publisher assumes no responsibility for errors or omissions, or for damages resulting from the use of the information contained herein.

THE GREEN ROUTE: DISCOVERING THE WORLD SUSTAINABLY

First edition. March 6, 2024.

ISBN: 979-8224575244

Written by Estelle-Maria Reed.

Table of Contents

Chapter 1: Getting Green Started – The Art of Sustainable Packing......1

Chapter 2: On the Go – Flying, Driving, Gliding? 7

Chapter 3: Sleeping with a Green Conscience 11

Chapter 4: Eating (and Drinking) for the Planet 13

Chapter 5: Encounters of the Sustainable Kind........................ 17

Chapter 6: Pure Nature – But Please, Responsibly........................ 21

Chapter 7: Riding the Green Wave – Eco-Adventures Worldwide 25

Chapter 8: Souvenirs That Don't Scream "I Was Here!" 29

Chapter 9: Digital Nomads – Green Working on the Go 33

Chapter 10: Voluntourism – Helping or Hindering? 39

Chapter 11: The Economics of Travel – Money That Does Good 43

Chapter 12: The Green Thumb – Environmental Projects for Travelers 51

Chapter 13: Sustainability at Sea – Cruises and Alternatives 55

Chapter 14: Saving the World – One Selfie at a Time............................ 57

Chapter 15: Rediscovering Cities – Urban Oases and Green Getaways.. 61

Chapter 16: The Great Silence – Retreats and Their Green Side 65

Chapter 17: Footprint-Free Festivals – Can It Be Done? 69

Chapter 18: Traveling Athletic – Experiencing the World with Muscle Power 73

Chapter 19: The Future of Travel – A Green Horizon............................77

Chapter 20: The Green Compass – How to Live Sustainably at Home Too 81

"The Green Route: Discovering the World Sustainably"

GETTING GREEN STARTED – The Art of Sustainable Packing

Chapter 1: Getting Green Started – The Art of Sustainable Packing

Ah, the art of packing light and minimizing waste while gallivanting across the globe sustainably – it's akin to performing a well-rehearsed ballet, except your audience is the planet, and every move is a step towards preserving its majestic beauty. You see, the philosophy behind packing light is not merely about avoiding excess baggage fees (though, let's admit, that's a pleasant perk). It's about treading lightly on the Earth, leaving no more than footprints behind, preferably those of a size that wouldn't embarrass a hobbit.

Minimizing waste, on the other hand, is an exercise in elegance and restraint, much like choosing the perfect words for a sonnet. It's about recognizing that every item we cavalierly toss into our bags has a lifecycle – a beginning, middle, and an all-too-often ignoble end in a landfill, where it languishes, contributing neither to aesthetics nor the well-being of our planet.

Traveling sustainably, by packing light and minimizing waste, is a testament to our respect for the destinations we are privileged to visit. It's an acknowledgment that these places are not merely backdrops for our selfies, but living, breathing ecosystems that demand our care and consideration. By choosing to pack only what we need and ensuring that we leave behind as little waste as possible, we're not just lightening our physical load but, more importantly, the burden we place on the environment.

Moreover, this approach to travel encourages a certain resourcefulness and creativity, much like a poet conjuring vivid imagery with a limited lexicon. It challenges us to find multiple uses for a single item, to forego the disposable for the durable, and to embrace the local and the sustainable. In doing so, we become not just travelers but stewards of the earth, participating in a grand tradition of exploration that honors the places and people we encounter.

So, my dear fellow wanderers, let us pack our bags with care, choosing each item as if it were a word in a beautiful narrative. Let's write a story of travel that's not only about the places we've seen but about the gentle marks we've left upon them – a tale of light footsteps and minimal waste, a testament to our love for this wondrous planet we call home.

Packing sustainably, you see, is akin to composing a symphony where every item plays its part harmoniously, contributing to the greater good of our planet. Let's embark on this melodious journey of packing, shall we?

Choosing Eco-Friendly Luggage: Begin with the maestro of your travel symphony – your luggage. Opt for bags made from recycled or sustainable materials. Brands that tout ethical manufacturing processes or support environmental initiatives take center stage here. Think of it as choosing the lead violinist for their skill as well as their harmony with the orchestra.

A Wardrobe That Whispers 'Sustainability': In the ensemble of your travel gear, clothing is the string section – versatile, essential, and numerous. Favor items made from organic, recycled, or upcycled fabrics. Clothes that can perform a duet, serving multiple purposes or suitable for various occasions, ensure you travel light and reduce the need for frequent laundering. The art lies in the selection of pieces that not only mix and match but also sing the praises of sustainability.

Reusable Toiletries – The Flautists of the Group: Delicate yet impactful, reusable toiletries play their tune softly but significantly. Solid shampoos, conditioners, and soaps skip the plastic packaging, as do bamboo toothbrushes and refillable razors. They're the flute's gentle trill amidst the orchestra's roar, reminding us that beauty routines need not be wasteful.

Multipurpose Marvels – The Brass Section: Just as the brass section adds depth and power, multipurpose items add weight (figuratively, not literally) to your sustainable packing list. A scarf that moonlights as a blanket, a sarong, or a picnic mat; a single, durable water bottle with a built-in filter; utensils and a container for impromptu meals – these are your trombones and trumpets, boldly declaring your commitment to sustainability.

The Rhythm Section – Bags and Containers: Keeping the beat, and your belongings organized, are reusable bags and containers. Silicone bags, collapsible food containers, and beeswax wraps keep your rhythm eco-friendly, reducing reliance on single-use plastics. Their steady beat underlines your travel melody.

Electronics – The Electronic Keyboards of the Orchestra: Essential yet energy-consuming, our electronic devices are like the synthesizers of the music world. Opt for solar-powered chargers and power banks, and remember to unplug chargers when not in use. Their harmonious integration ensures the orchestra's modern relevance, just as eco-friendly practices ensure our planet's future vibrancy.

The Conductor – You: Ultimately, the conductor of this symphony is you. Your choices, from the eco-friendly luggage that sets the stage to the reusable items that compose the melody, determine the sustainability of your travel. By choosing wisely, you lead your travel orchestra to perform a masterpiece that's as beautiful for the planet as it is for your soul.

In crafting this symphony of sustainable packing, remember that each choice, no matter how small, contributes to a larger harmony – a world where travel and sustainability play a duet that resonates for generations to come.

Ah, the delightful spectrum of travel, ranging from the rugged, earthy tones of backpacking to the opulent, high notes of luxury travel – each requires its own unique symphony of packing strategies, doesn't it? Let's compose these packing lists with the finesse of adapting a Shakespearean sonnet into a modern-day epic.

For the Intrepid Backpacker:

Overture of Minimalism: Begin with a lightweight, durable backpack as your vessel. Its fabric should whisper tales of resilience and sustainability.

Aria of Versatility: Clothing that performs across acts – quick-dry, layerable items that can take you from the chill of dawn to the warmth of midday. Think of it as your travel wardrobe performing a ballet, each piece gracefully complementing the next.

Concerto of Compactness: Miniature, multi-use toiletries, perhaps solid shampoos and conditioners, which not only save space but serenade the environment with their lack of plastic.

Sonnet of Survival: A compact first-aid kit, a multi-tool that's as adept at opening bottles as it is at fixing loose screws, and a headlamp – the spotlight illuminating your adventures.

Chorus of Connectivity: Keep electronic essentials harmonized with nature; think solar chargers and waterproof cases. Their melody keeps you connected without skipping the beat of adventure.

For the Luxury Traveler:

THE GREEN ROUTE: DISCOVERING THE WORLD SUSTAINABLY

Prelude to Elegance: Select luggage that speaks of both quality and sustainability – perhaps a piece crafted from recycled materials that still radiates luxury.

Ballad of the Wardrobe: Curate a collection of outfits that blend comfort with style, each piece echoing the theme of your destination. Silk scarves, lightweight blazers, and versatile evening wear that can dance through cocktail hours and gala dinners alike.

Rhapsody of Reusables: Even in luxury, the refrain of sustainability plays on. Opt for chic, reusable travel bottles for your toiletries, and don't forget a stylish water bottle to keep hydration close at hand.

Harmony of Health and Wellness: A well-stocked, elegant travel wellness kit – think rejuvenating face masks, essential oils, and perhaps an indulgent, compact skincare regimen to ensure you arrive glowing, regardless of time zones.

Serenade of Tech: For the luxury traveler, tech plays the role of enhancing the experience – noise-cancelling headphones for serene flights, the latest e-reader loaded with novels and travel guides, and perhaps a compact, high-quality camera to capture the journey's opulence.

In essence, whether you're the bard of the backcountry or the symphonist of the suite, the key to packing lies in harmonizing your essentials with the nature of your journey. Each item, from the rugged to the refined, should resonate with the purpose of your travels, creating a melody that enhances the experience, sustains the environment, and, most importantly, sings to your soul. So pack with intention, dear traveler, and let your journey's packing list be a prelude to the adventure that awaits.

On the Go – Flying, Driving, Gliding?

Chapter 2: On the Go – Flying, Driving, Gliding?

Ah, the quest for exploring the vast tapestry of our world often leads us to ponder the chariots we choose on our journey. Each mode of transportation, like instruments in an orchestra, contributes its unique tone to the symphony of environmental impact. Let us embark on an enlightening exploration of these various conveyances, shall we?

Airplanes, those magnificent birds of the industrial age, sing the highest notes in the carbon footprint scale. Their siren songs traverse continents and oceans with ease, yet their melody is bittersweet. For each kilometer flown, they release a choir of greenhouse gases into the atmosphere, not just CO_2 but also water vapor, contrails, and other emissions that play a significant role in climate change. The aria of air travel is both powerful and poignant, reminding us of the delicate balance between human aspiration and planetary health.

Automobiles, the soloists of personal freedom, and their larger cousins, buses, offer a more grounded accompaniment to the travel ensemble. Their environmental impact varies widely, singing a range of notes depending on the fuel efficiency, occupancy, and type of fuel used. Electric vehicles (EVs) hum a lower, gentler tune, especially when their batteries are charged with renewable energy, offering a hopeful melody for future travels.

Trains, those stalwart basses of the transportation family, offer one of the more environmentally harmonious options, particularly electric trains powered by sustainable energy sources. Their deep, steady rhythm allows for the movement of many passengers with a significantly lower carbon footprint per capita. Like a reliable bassline that supports a symphony, trains provide a foundation for sustainable travel over land.

Ah, the sweet, clear notes of bicycles and walking – the altos of our travel choir. These modes of transportation emit not a whisper of greenhouse gases, moving in harmony with nature's rhythms. They remind us of the joy of moving at a human pace, allowing us to savor the world's beauty up close. In cities and regions where these methods are viable, they compose a melody of sustainability and health, a testament to the possibilities of low-impact travel.

The realm of water travel is witnessing the rise of new tenors: electric and hybrid boats. While traditional maritime vessels have long belted out some of the heavier environmental impacts, these newcomers offer a more optimistic tune. As technology advances, the dream of sailing the seas with minimal harm to the watery depths becomes ever more attainable.

In the grand composition of our travels, each choice of transportation adds its voice to the chorus of environmental impact. As conscious travelers, we are the conductors of this orchestra, tasked with the challenge of harmonizing our desire to explore with our responsibility to the Earth. By choosing our modes of transportation wisely, we can compose a more sustainable and beautiful future for all.

In the grand journey of reducing our environmental footprints, each step, wheel turn, or flight path we choose can lead to a more harmonious relationship with our planet. Like composers keen on reducing the cacophony of dissonance, we can orchestrate our travels with mindfulness towards carbon emissions. Here's how to fine-tune your travel symphony to a more eco-friendly composition.

THE GREEN ROUTE: DISCOVERING THE WORLD SUSTAINABLY

Choosing direct flights can significantly lower emissions by reducing the need for the energy-intensive takeoffs and landings. Think of it as opting for a straight, uninterrupted melody rather than a complex fugue with multiple entries and exits.

Embracing buses, trains, and subways connects you with the local rhythm while emitting fewer greenhouse gases per capita. It's akin to a choir where each voice blends into a rich, unified harmony, showcasing how collective action leads to significant impact.

Every kilogram counts when flying. Packing lightly not only eases your burden but also the plane's fuel consumption. Imagine your luggage as notes on a stave; the fewer and lighter the notes, the more lilting the tune.

Traveling during off-peak times can reduce your carbon footprint by ensuring fuller flights and trains, optimizing their fuel usage. It's like finding the syncopation in music that adds depth and complexity to the overall harmony.

Alternative Eco-Friendly Transportation Options:

Renting or sharing an electric vehicle for road trips plays a soft, smooth tune in the travel orchestra, especially when charged with renewable energy. It offers the freedom of personal transportation with a significantly reduced environmental impact.

Bicycles, the silent heroes of eco-friendly travel, produce zero emissions and offer a heart-healthy way to explore. It's the delicate tinkle of bicycle bells that adds a joyful note to the urban soundscape, inviting us to slow down and appreciate the scenery.

Exploring a city or countryside on foot is perhaps the most intimate way to travel. Each step is a gentle pluck on the strings of a vast environmental symphony, creating a tactile connection with the earth beneath your feet.

For those drawn to the open sea, sailing emerges as an eco-friendly option, powered by the timeless and renewable energy of the wind. It's the natural crescendo of wind against sail, a testament to humanity's ancient harmony with the forces of nature.

Opting for hybrid or electric public transportation where available is like joining an innovative ensemble, pioneering the future of travel music. These options reduce reliance on fossil fuels, playing a crucial part in the transition to a greener travel narrative.

As travelers, we hold the baton and have the power to compose a more sustainable melody in our journeys. By making conscious choices and embracing eco-friendly transportation options, we can create a symphony of travel that harmonizes with the Earth's needs. Let us embark on this grand adventure, where the destination is not just a place but a future where our travels leave behind a softer, more beautiful footprint.

Sleeping with a Green Conscience

Chapter 3: Sleeping with a Green Conscience

In our quest to travel sustainably, one crucial aspect that often gets overlooked is the choice of accommodations. Where we choose to rest our weary heads at the end of a day of exploration can have a significant impact on our environmental footprint. By opting for eco-friendly accommodations, we can minimize waste, conserve natural resources, and reduce our carbon footprint. But the importance of choosing sustainable accommodations goes beyond just environmental considerations. It also supports conservation efforts, promotes sustainable practices in the hospitality industry, preserves local cultures, and contributes to the economic well-being of the communities we visit.

There are various types of sustainable accommodations that cater to different preferences and travel styles. Eco-lodges, for example, are nestled within natural settings, seamlessly blending into their surroundings while focusing on environmental conservation. Green hotels, on the other hand, are certified for their sustainable operations, from energy efficiency to water conservation. Bio-farms offer guests the opportunity to participate in organic farming and sustainable living, while eco-campsites promote minimal impact camping in pristine natural environments. Sustainable homestays and Airbnbs provide a more localized and sustainable experience, with energy-efficient homes that reflect the culture and values of the community.

Finding and booking sustainable accommodations may seem like a daunting task, but with a few tips and tricks, it becomes much more manageable. One crucial aspect to consider is certification. Look for accommodations that have credible sustainability certifications, such as Green Key or LEED, as these indicate a commitment to eco-friendly practices. It's also essential to do thorough research and read guest reviews to get a sense of the accommodation's sustainability practices and whether they align with your values.

When in doubt, don't hesitate to reach out directly to the accommodation and inquire about their environmental policies and practices. This direct contact allows you to gain a deeper understanding of their commitment to sustainability and can help you make an informed decision. Additionally, there are specialized websites like Ecobnb or BookDifferent that focus on eco-friendly stays, making it easier to find and book sustainable accommodations.

When considering sustainable accommodations, it's important to prioritize local and seasonal options. Look for accommodations that use local materials, serve local food, and are suitable for the climate. This not only supports the local economy but also reduces the carbon footprint associated with transportation and sourcing materials from afar. Pay attention to water and energy conservation practices, such as rainwater harvesting, solar panels, and energy-efficient lighting. Waste management is another crucial factor to consider, so opt for accommodations with comprehensive recycling programs and a commitment to minimizing single-use plastics.

By choosing eco-friendly accommodations, we can sleep with a green conscience, knowing that our travel choices are contributing to a more sustainable world. These accommodations not only provide us with a comfortable place to rest but also serve as a gateway to experiencing the beauty and culture of a destination in a way that respects and preserves the environment. So, let us embark on our journey with a commitment to sustainable travel, one accommodation at a time.

Eating (and Drinking) for the Planet

Chapter 4: Eating (and Drinking) for the Planet

In this chapter, we delve into the realm of sustainable eating while traveling and how our food choices can have a profound impact on the environment. From the carbon footprint of our meals to the land and water use involved, it is crucial to understand the consequences of our culinary decisions.

When it comes to eating sustainably while traveling, there are several tips and tricks that can make a significant difference. First and foremost, embracing local flavors is key. By frequenting local markets and eateries, we not only support the local economy but also reduce transportation emissions. The farm-to-table concept becomes a reality as we savor the freshest, tastiest produce that hasn't traveled thousands of miles to reach our plates.

Additionally, opting for seasonal selections is a sustainable choice. Seasonal produce not only boasts enhanced flavors but also has a smaller environmental footprint. With reduced needs for storage and transportation, these fruits and vegetables contribute to a more sustainable food system.

In our quest for sustainable eating, it is essential to consider the packaging of our food. Choosing items with minimal packaging helps reduce plastic waste and overall waste production. Whenever possible, bringing our own containers and utensils can further minimize our ecological impact.

Supporting organic options is another way to eat sustainably while traveling. Organic farming practices are designed to reduce pollution and conserve water, making them an environmentally friendly choice. By opting for organic offerings, we contribute to the preservation of our planet's delicate ecosystems.

One of the most impactful choices we can make for the environment is to prioritize plant-based meals. Plant-based diets generally have a lower environmental impact compared to meat-based diets. Exploring the local vegetarian cuisine not only reduces our carbon footprint but also introduces us to a myriad of new flavors and culinary experiences.

Water wisdom is also crucial when it comes to sustainable eating. Instead of buying bottled water, carrying a reusable water bottle can significantly reduce plastic waste. By making this simple switch, we can contribute to a more sustainable future.

Now, let's explore the realm of alternative protein sources, such as insect protein. Insects are a highly sustainable protein source, rich in nutrients and requiring far less land, water, and feed than traditional livestock. They have long been a part of many traditional cuisines around the world, and it's time for us to embrace their potential.

To explore alternative protein sources like insects, we can start by visiting local markets where insect dishes are sold. This allows us to try prepared insect-based foods in a culturally authentic way, immersing ourselves in the local culinary scene.

Specialty restaurants that specialize in contemporary or traditional dishes incorporating insects are another avenue to explore. Talented chefs often have creative ways of preparing insects that might surprise and delight our taste buds.

THE GREEN ROUTE: DISCOVERING THE WORLD SUSTAINABLY

For those seeking a more hands-on experience, participating in cooking classes that focus on local, sustainable cooking, including the use of insects, can be an enlightening adventure. Not only do we learn about this alternative protein source, but we also gain valuable skills and knowledge that we can carry with us on our journey.

In some regions, packaged insect protein products like cricket flour or energy bars can be found. These familiar formats provide an accessible introduction to insect protein, allowing us to ease into this sustainable protein source at our own pace.

Our food choices while traveling have a significant impact on the environment. By embracing local flavors, opting for seasonal selections, minimizing packaging, supporting organic options, prioritizing plant-based meals, and exploring alternative protein sources like insects, we can eat sustainably and contribute to a more sustainable future for our planet. Let us embark on this gastronomic journey, savoring the flavors of the world while treading lightly on the Earth.

Encounters of the Sustainable Kind

Chapter 5: Encounters of the Sustainable Kind

In the realm of sustainable travel, there exists a profound opportunity for travelers to engage with local cultures and communities in a way that is not only enriching for themselves but also beneficial for the destinations and their inhabitants. It is a chance to transcend the role of a mere observer and become an active participant in the tapestry of a new culture. But how does one navigate this delicate dance of cultural exchange with grace and sensitivity? In this chapter, we will explore the art of engaging with local cultures sustainably and delve into the transformative power of meaningful encounters.

To embark on a journey of cultural immersion, one must first approach it with a deep respect for the customs and traditions of the places they visit. It is a dance of understanding, where research and knowledge become the guiding steps. By taking the time to learn about the cultural norms, traditions, and taboos of a destination, travelers can ensure that their actions are in harmony with the local way of life. Whether it is respecting dress codes, following etiquette, or observing sacred customs, this foundation of respect sets the stage for a meaningful exchange.

But engaging with local cultures goes beyond mere observation. It is about actively supporting the communities that call these destinations home. By choosing locally owned accommodations, restaurants, and tour operators, travelers can contribute to the local economy and ensure that their money stays within the community. It is a symbiotic relationship, where the traveler receives an authentic experience, and the community benefits from the economic empowerment that sustainable tourism brings.

Language, too, plays a pivotal role in the dance of cultural exchange. Even if it is just a few basic phrases, making an effort to learn the local language demonstrates respect for the culture and opens doors to meaningful interactions. It is the bridge that connects hearts and minds, allowing for a deeper understanding of the local way of life.

Participating in cultural activities further deepens the connection between traveler and destination. Attending festivals, performances, and cultural events not only provides insight into the local way of life but also contributes to the preservation of traditional arts and heritage. It is a celebration of the rich tapestry of human expression, where the traveler becomes an active participant in the preservation of cultural treasures.

Volunteering responsibly is another avenue through which travelers can engage with local communities sustainably. By seeking out opportunities that benefit the community and environment, travelers can ensure that their actions align with the actual needs of the community and do not disrupt local livelihoods. It is a chance to give back, to contribute to the well-being of the places we visit, and to leave a positive impact in our wake.

But sustainable engagement goes beyond the human realm. It is also about minimizing our environmental footprint. Responsible tourism means reducing waste, conserving water and energy, and opting for eco-friendly transportation options whenever possible. It is a commitment to treading lightly on the earth, ensuring that future generations can also experience the wonders of the world.

Engaging with locals is the heartbeat of sustainable travel. It is through conversations, questions, and genuine interest that cultural exchanges are born. By striking up conversations with locals, travelers can gain a deeper understanding of their culture, their way of life, and their hopes and dreams. It is a chance to bridge the gap between traveler and local, to find common ground amidst the beautiful diversity of our world.

THE GREEN ROUTE: DISCOVERING THE WORLD SUSTAINABLY

Respecting natural and cultural heritage is another essential aspect of sustainable engagement. It is a call to treat the places we visit with care and respect, to follow designated trails, avoid littering, and refrain from damaging or removing artifacts. It is a recognition that these sites hold immense value, not just for the present generation but for generations to come.

Community-based tourism initiatives offer yet another avenue for sustainable engagement. By seeking out projects that empower local communities and provide sustainable livelihoods, travelers can experience authentic cultural experiences while directly benefiting the local people. It is a chance to immerse oneself in the fabric of a community, to learn from its people, and to support their aspirations for a better future.

Finally, education serves as the foundation upon which sustainable engagement is built. By taking the time to learn about the social, economic, and environmental issues facing the communities we visit, we can make informed choices and contribute positively to sustainable development efforts. It is an ongoing journey of understanding, where knowledge becomes the catalyst for change.

Engaging with local cultures and communities in a sustainable way is a transformative experience. It is a dance of respect, support, and understanding, where the traveler becomes an active participant in the preservation of cultural heritage and the empowerment of local communities. By following these guidelines, travelers can embark on a journey of meaningful encounters, where the world becomes their classroom and the people they meet become their teachers. It is a path of discovery, where the traveler and the destination are forever intertwined in a dance of sustainability and shared humanity.

Pure Nature – But Please, Responsibly

Chapter 6: Pure Nature – But Please, Responsibly

As travelers, we are fortunate to have the opportunity to explore and connect with the natural world. From breathtaking landscapes to diverse wildlife, nature offers us a sense of wonder and awe. However, with this privilege comes the responsibility to ensure that our presence does not harm or disrupt the delicate balance of these ecosystems. In this chapter, we will delve into the importance of visiting natural and conservation areas responsibly, and explore some practical tips on how to minimize our impact on wildlife and ecosystems.

When embarking on a journey to a natural or conservation area, it is crucial to research and plan ahead. Familiarize yourself with the rules, regulations, and guidelines set by park authorities or local conservation organizations. This knowledge will help you understand what activities are permitted and how to minimize your impact on the environment. By staying on designated trails, you can avoid damaging fragile ecosystems and disturbing wildlife habitats. Venturing off-trail can trample vegetation, erode soil, and disrupt animal habitats. Remember, the path less traveled is not always the path to take.

Leave No Trace – these three words hold immense significance when exploring nature. Practice Leave No Trace principles by packing out all trash, including food wrappers, cigarette butts, and other waste. Leave the area as you found it, or even better, pick up any litter you find along the way. By doing so, you not only prevent pollution but also show respect for the environment and for future visitors.

Respecting wildlife is another crucial aspect of responsible nature exploration. Observe wildlife from a safe distance and avoid feeding or approaching animals. Keep noise levels to a minimum to minimize disturbance to wildlife and their natural behaviors. Remember, we are merely guests in their home, and it is our duty to ensure their safety and well-being.

Campfires, a quintessential part of outdoor experiences, can also have a significant impact on the environment if not used responsibly. If campfires are permitted, use designated fire rings or stoves and follow local regulations for fire safety. Use only dead wood for fires and completely extinguish them before leaving the area. By doing so, you protect the surrounding vegetation and prevent the risk of wildfires.

Water, the essence of life, should be conserved even in the midst of nature's abundance. Practice water conservation by using it sparingly for drinking, cooking, and cleaning. Avoid contaminating water sources with soaps, detergents, or other pollutants. By doing your part to conserve water, you contribute to the sustainability of these ecosystems and ensure their longevity.

Sensitive wildlife habitats, such as nesting areas, breeding grounds, or migratory routes, should be respected and left undisturbed. Avoid camping, picnicking, or hiking in these areas. They are critical for the survival of many species and should be protected from human interference. By doing so, you allow nature to thrive and maintain its delicate balance.

Educating yourself about the flora, fauna, and ecosystems of the area you are visiting is not only enriching but also essential for responsible exploration. Understanding the natural environment enhances your appreciation for it and helps you make informed decisions about how to minimize your impact. Share your knowledge with others and encourage them to practice responsible and sustainable outdoor recreation.

THE GREEN ROUTE: DISCOVERING THE WORLD SUSTAINABLY

Supporting conservation efforts is not just an option but a responsibility. By donating to local conservation organizations or volunteering for conservation projects in the area, you contribute to the preservation and protection of natural areas for future generations to enjoy. Your support helps maintain biodiversity, sustain ecosystem services, and promote sustainable development.

Lastly, be considerate of others who share your love for nature. Keep noise levels down, yield to hikers on narrow trails, and practice good trail etiquette. Everyone deserves to enjoy the beauty of nature without disruption. By respecting the experiences of others, you contribute to a harmonious and enjoyable environment for all.

Visiting natural and conservation areas is a privilege that comes with great responsibility. By following these guidelines, you can explore the wonders of nature while minimizing your impact on wildlife and ecosystems. Let us be stewards of the environment, ensuring that these precious landscapes and their inhabitants thrive for generations to come.

Riding the Green Wave – Eco-Adventures Worldwide

Chapter 7: Riding the Green Wave – Eco-Adventures Worldwide

In the realm of sustainable travel, supporting conservation efforts while embarking on adventurous journeys is crucial. The reasons for this are manifold. Firstly, biodiversity conservation is of paramount importance. Many travel destinations are home to diverse ecosystems and endangered species. By supporting conservation efforts, travelers can play a role in protecting these habitats and the biodiversity they contain.

Furthermore, environmental protection is a pressing concern in the realm of travel and tourism. Activities such as habitat destruction, pollution, and overconsumption of resources can have detrimental effects on the environment. By supporting conservation initiatives, travelers can help mitigate these impacts and promote sustainable practices.

Sustainable development is another key aspect of conservation efforts. By involving local communities in conservation projects, travelers can contribute to their economic development. This, in turn, reduces their dependence on harmful activities such as logging or poaching.

Cultural preservation is closely intertwined with conservation efforts. Many projects that protect natural resources also work towards preserving cultural heritage and traditions. By supporting these initiatives, travelers can contribute to the preservation of unique cultural identities and traditions.

Ecotourism opportunities abound in conservation areas. Many of these areas offer eco-friendly experiences that allow travelers to explore natural landscapes while supporting conservation efforts financially. By participating in these activities, travelers directly contribute to the protection and preservation of these areas.

Lastly, conservation efforts play a significant role in mitigating the impacts of climate change. By protecting carbon sinks like forests and wetlands, these efforts help reduce greenhouse gas emissions and build resilience to climate change.

When it comes to sustainable adventure travel options, hiking and kayaking are excellent choices. Hiking enthusiasts should choose well-maintained and designated trails to minimize their environmental impact. Practicing Leave No Trace principles, such as packing out all trash and staying on designated trails, is essential. Joining guided hikes led by local experts who can provide insights into the natural and cultural history of the area is also highly recommended.

For those who prefer kayaking, exploring rivers, lakes, and coastlines by kayak offers a unique way to experience nature up close while minimizing environmental impact. Opting for eco-friendly kayaking operators that adhere to sustainable practices is crucial. These practices may include using non-motorized boats, avoiding sensitive habitats, and educating participants about local ecosystems. Participating in kayaking tours that support conservation initiatives, such as river clean-up efforts or wildlife monitoring projects, is an excellent way to contribute to environmental protection.

Personal stories and exciting adventures from eco-adventures are abundant. One such story takes us to the lush rainforests of Costa Rica. Imagine embarking on a guided hike through the dense canopy of the Monteverde Cloud Forest Reserve. Towering trees draped in moss form a verdant cathedral overhead. The misty trails are teeming with life, and the symphony of sounds emanating from the forest floor is overwhelming. The melodious calls of tropical birds, the rhythmic chirping of crickets, and the gentle rustle of leaves create a sensory experience like no other. A knowledgeable guide leads a small group through the tangled undergrowth, pointing out hidden treasures along the way. Iridescent butterflies, elusive sloths, and colorful frogs add to the enchantment. The journey takes us deeper into the heart of the rainforest, where a hidden waterfall awaits. Its crystal-clear waters shimmer in the dappled sunlight, inviting us to plunge into its cool embrace. This eco-adventure is not just an exploration of the natural world; it is also a journey of self-discovery, a reminder of the interconnectedness of all living things and the importance of preserving our planet's precious ecosystems.

Another thrilling eco-adventure takes us to Tortuguero National Park in Costa Rica. Kayaking along the winding rivers, surrounded by dense mangroves, brings us face to face with a dazzling array of wildlife. Playful river otters and elusive jaguars are just a few of the creatures that call this pristine wilderness home. Each paddle stroke reveals a new marvel waiting to be discovered. From nesting sea turtles on remote beaches to vibrant toucans perched high above the canopy, the wonders of nature unfold at every turn. As the sun sets and the sky blazes with hues of orange and gold, the realization dawns that this eco-adventure is not only an exploration of the natural world but also a journey of self-discovery and a reminder of the importance of preserving our planet's precious ecosystems.

Eco-adventures offer a unique and sustainable way to explore the world. By supporting conservation efforts, choosing eco-friendly activities, and immersing ourselves in the wonders of nature, we can make a positive impact while creating unforgettable memories. Let us ride the green wave of eco-adventures and discover the world sustainably.

ESTELLE-MARIA REED

Souvenirs That Don't Scream "I Was Here!"

Chapter 8: Souvenirs That Don't Scream "I Was Here!"

———

In the bustling markets and artisanal shops of the world, travelers often find themselves surrounded by an array of souvenirs, each vying for their attention. But amidst the sea of trinkets and mass-produced mementos, how can one choose a souvenir that truly reflects their journey, without leaving a negative impact on the environment or local communities? In this chapter, we will explore the art of selecting sustainable and ethical souvenirs that don't scream "I was here!" but instead whisper stories of cultural heritage, craftsmanship, and environmental stewardship.

When it comes to choosing sustainable and ethical souvenirs, there are several key principles to keep in mind. First and foremost, supporting local artisans is crucial. Look for souvenirs that are handmade by local craftspeople, using traditional techniques and locally sourced materials. By purchasing directly from artisans, you not only support local economies but also help preserve traditional craftsmanship that is often at risk of being lost in the face of mass production.

Another important factor to consider is the materials used in the production of the souvenir. Opt for items made from sustainable and eco-friendly materials, such as bamboo, recycled glass, organic cotton, or reclaimed wood. Avoid products made from endangered or non-renewable resources, such as ivory, coral, or tropical hardwoods. By choosing souvenirs made from sustainable materials, you contribute to the conservation of natural resources and reduce your ecological footprint.

It is also crucial to avoid purchasing souvenirs made from wildlife or animal products. Items such as ivory, tortoiseshell, feathers, or fur contribute to illegal wildlife trafficking and threaten endangered species. Instead, choose souvenirs that celebrate the beauty of nature without harming it, such as botanical prints, handmade paper, or ethically sourced gemstones.

When shopping for souvenirs, be sure to check for Fair Trade certification. Fair Trade ensures that artisans receive fair wages and work in safe conditions. Look for products that carry the Fair Trade label or certification logo, indicating compliance with ethical standards. By supporting Fair Trade practices, you can make a positive impact on the lives of artisans and their communities.

Consider the environmental impact of the souvenir as well. Take into account its production process, packaging, and transportation. Choose items that are minimally packaged or packaged in recyclable materials to reduce waste. Additionally, opt for souvenirs that serve a practical purpose or are consumable, such as locally made crafts, artisanal foods, or natural skincare products. These items are less likely to end up as clutter and can be enjoyed without contributing to waste accumulation.

When purchasing souvenirs, don't hesitate to ask questions. Inquire about the product's origin, materials, and production process. Seek out retailers and artisans who are transparent about their sourcing and manufacturing practices. By being an informed consumer, you can make choices that align with your values and support sustainable and ethical practices.

Consider purchasing souvenirs from conservation organizations or visitor centers that support local conservation efforts. These souvenirs often feature wildlife-themed merchandise or educational materials that raise awareness about environmental issues. By supporting these organizations, you contribute to the preservation of natural habitats and the protection of endangered species.

Lastly, choose souvenirs that are authentic and meaningful. Look for items that reflect the local culture, traditions, and heritage of the destination. Choose souvenirs that have personal significance or tell a story, rather than mass-produced trinkets or generic souvenirs. By selecting souvenirs that are unique and reflective of the place you visited, you bring a piece of that experience back home with you, forever reminding you of the memories and connections you made.

Choosing sustainable and ethical souvenirs is not only an act of responsible travel but also a way to support local communities, preserve traditional craftsmanship, and promote environmental conservation. By following the tips and principles outlined in this chapter, travelers can make conscious choices that align with their values and leave a positive impact on the places they visit. So the next time you find yourself in a bustling market, remember to choose souvenirs that don't scream "I was here!" but instead whisper tales of sustainability, cultural heritage, and a world worth preserving.

Digital Nomads – Green Working on the Go

Chapter 9: Digital Nomads – Green Working on the Go

In today's fast-paced world, the concept of work has evolved beyond the confines of traditional office spaces. With the rise of remote work and digital nomadism, individuals have the freedom to work from anywhere in the world, untethered by the constraints of a physical office. But what does this mean for sustainability? Can remote work and digital nomadism coexist with a green lifestyle? In this chapter, we will explore the practices and experiences of digital nomads who prioritize sustainability in their work and travel.

Remote workers and digital nomads have a unique opportunity to make a positive impact on the environment through their work and lifestyle choices. By incorporating sustainable practices into their daily routines, they can minimize their environmental footprint and contribute to a greener future. From energy-efficient workspaces to eco-friendly transportation options, there are numerous ways for digital nomads to work sustainably on the go.

One of the key aspects of sustainable remote work is creating an energy-efficient workspace. By using LED lighting, energy-efficient appliances, and power-saving settings on electronic devices, digital nomads can reduce their energy consumption. Additionally, considering renewable energy sources like solar power or wind energy can further enhance the sustainability of their workspace.

Another important practice for digital nomads is to minimize paper usage. Instead of printing out documents, opting for digital documents, e-signatures, and online collaboration tools can significantly reduce paper waste. Digital notebooks or cloud-based note-taking apps also provide a sustainable alternative for jotting down ideas and taking notes.

Furthermore, digital nomads can minimize their environmental impact by reducing commuting. Taking advantage of remote work opportunities and working from home, nearby coworking spaces, or coffee shops can help minimize carbon emissions. By choosing eco-friendly transportation options such as walking, biking, or using public transportation, digital nomads can further reduce their carbon footprint while traveling.

Waste reduction is another crucial aspect of sustainable remote work. Minimizing the use of single-use items like plastic bottles, utensils, and packaging can significantly reduce waste. Opting for reusable water bottles, coffee cups, and food containers, as well as choosing products with minimal or recyclable packaging, can make a significant difference.

Conserving water and energy is also important for digital nomads. By taking shorter showers, turning off lights and electronics when not in use, and adjusting the thermostat to conserve energy, digital nomads can contribute to water and energy conservation in their accommodations.

When it comes to choosing accommodations and coworking spaces, digital nomads can prioritize sustainability by considering eco-friendly options. Researching sustainable coworking spaces that prioritize energy-efficient buildings, recycling programs, and eco-friendly amenities is essential. Looking for recognized green certifications such as LEED or BREEAM can ensure that the space meets high environmental standards. Likewise, choosing eco-friendly accommodations with energy-efficient appliances, water-saving measures, and eco-friendly certifications can further support sustainability efforts.

THE GREEN ROUTE: DISCOVERING THE WORLD SUSTAINABLY

Eating locally and sustainably is another way for digital nomads to contribute to a greener world. Supporting local farmers and reducing carbon footprint by eating locally sourced and sustainably produced food can have a positive impact on both the environment and local communities. Visiting farmers' markets, grocery stores, and restaurants that prioritize local, organic, and seasonal ingredients is a great way to embrace sustainable eating habits.

Offsetting carbon emissions is another practice that digital nomads can consider. By investing in carbon offset programs or supporting reforestation and renewable energy projects, digital nomads can take responsibility for their carbon footprint and contribute to environmental conservation.

Lastly, digital nomads should prioritize work-life balance and self-care to maintain their well-being and prevent burnout. Taking regular breaks, getting plenty of exercise and fresh air, and making time for hobbies and leisure activities are essential for a sustainable and fulfilling work-life balance.

Incorporating these sustainable practices into their work and travel routines, digital nomads can lead by example and inspire others to embrace a greener way of living and working. By minimizing their environmental impact, supporting local communities, and promoting sustainability, digital nomads can pave the way for a more sustainable future.

Digital nomads have the unique opportunity to blend work and travel seamlessly, and in doing so, they can experience the world in a way that few others can. From working on the shores of a volcanic lake in Iceland to setting up a mobile office in remote highland valleys, the possibilities are endless.

One digital nomad recounts their experience of working remotely in Iceland, a land of rugged landscapes and awe-inspiring beauty. Armed with their laptop, camera, and a sense of adventure, they embarked on a journey across Iceland's countryside, setting up their mobile office in some of the country's most picturesque locations.

One of their most memorable experiences took place on the shores of Lake Myvatn, a volcanic lake in northern Iceland. With steam rising from the geothermal vents and the sound of bubbling mud pots in the background, they found the perfect spot to park their camper van and set up their workspace. From there, they were able to draw inspiration from the dramatic landscapes and ever-changing weather patterns, fueled by the sense of wonder and awe that surrounded them.

Between work sessions, they took breaks to explore hiking trails, soak in natural hot springs, and marvel at cascading waterfalls. They even had the opportunity to witness the mesmerizing spectacle of the Northern Lights dancing across the night sky, a sight that left them awestruck and humbled by the beauty of the natural world.

Throughout their journey, they worked from a variety of unique locations, each offering its own challenges and rewards. From secluded fjords and windswept cliffs to remote highland valleys and black sand beaches, they were able to blend work and travel seamlessly while being inspired by the breathtaking landscapes that surrounded them.

By the end of their remote working adventure in Iceland, they had not only met their deadlines and exceeded their clients' expectations but also gained a newfound appreciation for the power of remote work to connect us with the world around us. Their journey had been an unforgettable experience that left them longing for more adventures on the road.

THE GREEN ROUTE: DISCOVERING THE WORLD SUSTAINABLY

This story serves as a reminder of the unique opportunities and experiences that remote work can offer. It allows individuals to explore the world while maintaining their work responsibilities, all while embracing a sustainable and environmentally conscious lifestyle.

Digital nomads have the power to work sustainably and make a positive impact on the environment. By incorporating sustainable practices into their work and travel routines, they can minimize their environmental footprint, support local communities, and promote a greener way of living and working. Whether it's setting up an energy-efficient workspace, choosing eco-friendly transportation, or supporting sustainable accommodations, digital nomads can lead the way towards a more sustainable future. So, pack your laptop, embrace the nomadic lifestyle, and discover the world sustainably on the green route.

Voluntourism – Helping or Hindering?

Chapter 10: Voluntourism – Helping or Hindering?

Voluntourism, the combination of volunteering and travel, has gained popularity in recent years. It offers travelers the opportunity to make a positive impact while exploring new destinations. However, like any form of travel, voluntourism has its pros and cons. In this chapter, we will delve into the advantages and disadvantages of voluntourism and explore whether it truly helps or hinders the communities it aims to serve.

On the positive side, voluntourism allows travelers to make a meaningful contribution to local communities and projects. By volunteering their time and skills, they can support causes such as teaching, construction, conservation work, or healthcare assistance. This hands-on involvement provides a sense of fulfillment and allows volunteers to see the direct impact of their efforts.

Furthermore, voluntourism fosters cultural exchange and cross-cultural learning. Volunteers have the opportunity to engage with local communities, learn about their customs, traditions, and way of life, and gain a deeper understanding of global issues. This cultural immersion can be a transformative experience that broadens perspectives and cultivates empathy.

Voluntourism also promotes personal growth. Stepping outside one's comfort zone and engaging in meaningful work can lead to personal development, empathy, and a greater sense of social responsibility. Volunteers develop new skills, gain perspective on their own lives and privileges, and become more aware of global issues.

From a travel perspective, voluntourism offers a unique and immersive experience. It allows travelers to explore off-the-beaten-path locations, interact with locals, and gain insights into the daily lives of community members. This type of travel goes beyond typical tourist activities, providing a deeper connection to the destination.

Additionally, voluntourism can contribute to local economies. By supporting community-based projects, voluntourism provides income, supports small businesses, and creates employment opportunities for local guides, coordinators, and support staff. This economic impact can help foster sustainable development and empower local communities.

However, voluntourism also has its drawbacks. One of the main concerns is the short-term impact of volunteer projects. Due to their limited duration and the transient nature of volunteers, projects often lack continuity, sustainability, and meaningful outcomes. This can result in dependency on external assistance rather than empowering local communities.

Ethical concerns also arise in voluntourism. Motivations, qualifications, and impact of voluntourists can be questionable. Some projects may prioritize the experience of volunteers over the needs of local communities, perpetuate stereotypes, or exploit vulnerable populations for tourism purposes. It is crucial to critically assess the ethical implications of voluntourism.

Furthermore, voluntourism may sometimes prioritize the interests of volunteers or organizations over the actual needs of local communities. Projects may focus on feel-good activities or photo opportunities rather than addressing systemic issues and promoting sustainable development. This misplaced focus can hinder long-term progress.

Dependency issues are another challenge associated with voluntourism. Projects run the risk of creating dependency on external assistance, perpetuating a cycle of aid without fostering self-reliance and community empowerment. This can disempower community members and reinforce unequal power dynamics.

Lastly, voluntourism can have unintended consequences. Cultural disruption, environmental degradation, and displacement of local labor are some examples. It may also contribute to the commodification of poverty and reinforce stereotypes about developing countries. These unintended consequences must be carefully considered.

Voluntourism has the potential to make a positive impact and provide meaningful experiences for volunteers and host communities. However, it is essential to approach it with critical awareness, ethical considerations, and a focus on long-term sustainability and community empowerment. By doing so, voluntourism can truly become a force for positive change in the world.

The Economics of Travel – Money That Does Good

Chapter 11: The Economics of Travel – Money That Does Good

In this chapter, we will explore the economics of travel and how conscious spending can support local communities and promote sustainable tourism. Conscious spending, also known as mindful or ethical spending, plays a crucial role in creating a positive impact on the places we visit. By making mindful purchasing decisions that prioritize economic, environmental, and social sustainability, travelers can contribute to positive change and create meaningful experiences for themselves and others.

Supporting Local Businesses: When travelers consciously choose to spend their money at locally owned businesses, they directly contribute to the local economy. This helps create jobs, generate income for local residents, and support small-scale entrepreneurs, thereby strengthening the economic resilience of the community.

Preserving Cultural Heritage: Conscious spending helps preserve and promote traditional crafts, cultural practices, and heritage sites. By supporting local artisans, craftsmen, and cultural initiatives, travelers can contribute to the preservation of cultural identity and heritage.

Reducing Environmental Impact: Conscious spending encourages travelers to choose environmentally sustainable products and services that minimize their ecological footprint. By supporting eco-friendly accommodations, transportation providers, and tour operators, travelers can help reduce carbon emissions, conserve natural resources, and protect fragile ecosystems.

Fostering Community Engagement: Conscious spending fosters deeper connections between travelers and local communities, promoting authentic cultural exchange and mutual understanding. Engaging with local residents, learning about their customs, traditions, and way of life, and participating in community-based initiatives contribute to meaningful interactions and positive relationships between tourists and locals.

Promoting Social Responsibility: Conscious spending encourages travelers to consider the social impact of their purchasing decisions and support businesses that prioritize ethical practices, fair labor conditions, and community development initiatives. By choosing companies and products that adhere to responsible sourcing, fair trade, and corporate social responsibility principles, travelers can promote social justice and equitable development.

Empowering Local Communities: By investing in local businesses and community-based initiatives, conscious spending empowers local residents to take control of their own development and shape the future of their communities. Supporting grassroots organizations, cooperatives, and social enterprises enables communities to address their own needs, build capacity, and create sustainable livelihoods.

Encouraging Responsible Tourism Practices: Conscious spending sends a message to the tourism industry that travelers value sustainability, authenticity, and responsible tourism practices. By rewarding businesses that prioritize environmental and social responsibility with their patronage, travelers can encourage the adoption of sustainable practices and contribute to the transformation of the tourism industry as a whole.

In summary, conscious spending is a powerful tool for promoting sustainable tourism and supporting local communities. By making mindful purchasing decisions that prioritize economic, environmental, and social sustainability, travelers can contribute to positive change and create meaningful experiences for themselves and others.

Tips for Responsible Shopping and Supporting Local Businesses While Traveling

Responsible shopping while traveling involves making mindful purchasing decisions that support local businesses, promote sustainability, and minimize negative impacts on the environment and communities. Here are some tips for responsible shopping and supporting local businesses while traveling:

Research Local Businesses: Before you travel, research local businesses, artisans, and markets at your destination. Look for locally owned shops, boutiques, and craft markets that offer unique products and support the local economy.

Shop at Markets and Artisanal Fairs: Visit local markets, artisanal fairs, and craft cooperatives to purchase handmade crafts, artwork, and traditional products directly from local artisans and producers. These venues often offer a wide selection of authentic and locally made items while providing opportunities for cultural exchange and interaction with artisans.

Buy Authentic and Meaningful Souvenirs: Choose souvenirs that reflect the local culture, traditions, and heritage of the destination. Look for handmade crafts, textiles, pottery, and artwork that are unique to the region and have personal significance. Avoid mass-produced, generic souvenirs that lack authenticity and connection to the local culture.

Support Social Enterprises and Fair Trade Organizations: Seek out social enterprises, fair trade organizations, and community-based initiatives that prioritize ethical practices, fair wages, and community development. Look for certifications such as Fair Trade or local sustainability labels that indicate compliance with ethical standards.

Ask Questions and Engage with Sellers: Take the time to ask questions and engage with sellers, artisans, and producers to learn about the origin, production process, and cultural significance of the products you're interested in purchasing. Show genuine interest in their work, and respect their knowledge and expertise.

Choose Sustainable and Eco-friendly Products: Look for products that are made from sustainable materials, such as organic cotton, bamboo, or recycled materials. Avoid products that contribute to environmental degradation or exploitation of natural resources.

Reduce Single-Use Packaging: Minimize waste by choosing products with minimal or recyclable packaging. Bring reusable shopping bags, containers, and water bottles to avoid single-use plastic and packaging waste. Support businesses that offer refill stations or bulk options for reducing packaging waste.

Negotiate Fair Prices: When purchasing items at local markets or from independent sellers, negotiate fair prices that reflect the value of the product and the skill of the artisan. Respect cultural norms and bargaining practices, and avoid haggling excessively or exploiting sellers.

Leave Reviews and Recommendations: After your shopping experience, consider leaving positive reviews and recommendations for local businesses, artisans, and markets to help promote their products and services to other travelers. Share your shopping finds on social media and travel forums to inspire others to support local businesses.

Spread the Word: Share your shopping experiences and recommendations with friends, family, and fellow travelers to encourage responsible shopping and support for local businesses. By spreading the word about your favorite finds and highlighting the importance of responsible tourism, you can inspire others to make mindful purchasing decisions while traveling.

By following these tips for responsible shopping and supporting local businesses while traveling, you can contribute to sustainable tourism practices, promote economic empowerment, and foster meaningful connections with local communities and cultures.

Examples of Sustainable Tourism Initiatives that Benefit Local Economies

There are numerous sustainable tourism initiatives that benefit local economies. Here are some examples:

Community-Based Tourism: Community-based tourism initiatives involve local communities in the development, management, and promotion of tourism activities. By empowering communities to showcase their cultural heritage, traditions, and natural resources, community-based tourism creates economic opportunities for local residents, preserves cultural identity, and promotes sustainable development.

Fair Trade Tourism: Fair trade tourism initiatives aim to promote ethical practices, fair wages, and community development in the tourism industry. By partnering with fair trade-certified accommodations, tour operators, and souvenir shops, travelers can support businesses that prioritize social responsibility and equitable distribution of benefits.

Ecotourism: Ecotourism initiatives focus on promoting responsible travel to natural areas that conserve the environment, support local communities, and provide educational and recreational opportunities for visitors. By supporting ecotourism initiatives such as nature reserves, wildlife sanctuaries, and eco-lodges, travelers contribute to conservation efforts, create sustainable livelihoods for local residents, and promote environmental awareness and stewardship.

Agrotourism: Agrotourism initiatives involve visits to farms, vineyards, and rural estates where travelers can learn about agricultural practices, participate in farm activities, and sample local products. By supporting agrotourism initiatives, travelers contribute to rural economies, support small-scale farmers and producers, and promote sustainable agriculture and food systems.

Cultural Heritage Tourism: Cultural heritage tourism initiatives focus on preserving and promoting cultural landmarks, historical sites, and traditional practices while providing economic opportunities for local communities. By visiting cultural heritage sites, museums, and cultural events, travelers contribute to the preservation of cultural heritage, support heritage conservation efforts, and generate income for local artisans, performers, and cultural organizations.

Responsible Shopping Initiatives: Sustainable tourism initiatives encourage travelers to support local businesses, artisans, and cooperatives by purchasing locally made products, handicrafts, and souvenirs. By promoting responsible shopping practices and highlighting the value of authentic, locally sourced products, sustainable tourism initiatives create economic opportunities for artisans, preserve traditional crafts, and promote cultural exchange between travelers and local communities.

These examples demonstrate how sustainable tourism initiatives can have a positive impact on local economies by creating sustainable livelihoods, preserving cultural heritage, and promoting equitable distribution of benefits.

THE GREEN ROUTE: DISCOVERING THE WORLD SUSTAINABLY

The economics of travel extend beyond personal expenditure. By making conscious spending choices, travelers can support local communities, preserve cultural heritage, reduce environmental impact, foster community engagement, promote social responsibility, empower local communities, and encourage responsible tourism practices. Through responsible shopping and support for sustainable tourism initiatives, travelers can contribute to positive change and create meaningful experiences for themselves and others. So, let's embark on the green route and discover the world sustainably, one mindful purchase at a time.

The Green Thumb – Environmental Projects for Travelers

Chapter 12: The Green Thumb – Environmental Projects for Travelers

In a world where the fragility of our environment is becoming increasingly apparent, travelers have a unique opportunity to make a difference. By participating in environmental projects while traveling, they can contribute to conservation efforts, promote sustainability, and protect natural ecosystems. There are countless ways for travelers to get involved in these initiatives, and in this chapter, we will explore some of the most impactful ones.

One of the most direct ways to make a difference is by volunteering with conservation organizations. These organizations offer various opportunities for travelers to engage in environmental projects, such as wildlife monitoring, habitat restoration, and conservation research. Whether joining organized volunteer programs or reaching out directly to local conservation organizations, travelers can play a vital role in protecting the natural world.

Another avenue for travelers to contribute is through participating in ecotourism activities. By choosing tours and activities that promote environmental conservation and support local initiatives, travelers can learn about local ecosystems while promoting environmental awareness and appreciation. Activities like birdwatching, hiking, and snorkeling can foster a deeper connection with nature and inspire a sense of responsibility towards its preservation.

Beach cleanups and marine conservation projects provide another avenue for travelers to make a tangible impact. By participating in these initiatives, travelers can help protect coastal and marine ecosystems from pollution and degradation. Many coastal destinations offer organized beach cleanup events that welcome volunteers to participate in cleaning up litter and debris from beaches and shorelines.

Furthermore, travelers can get involved in reforestation and habitat restoration projects. By planting trees and restoring degraded ecosystems, they can promote biodiversity and combat deforestation. Whether joining reforestation projects, mangrove restoration efforts, or community-led conservation programs, travelers can actively contribute to the restoration of our planet's natural habitats.

Supporting sustainable agriculture is another way for travelers to make a difference. By participating in initiatives that promote environmentally friendly farming practices and support local food systems, travelers can contribute to the preservation of natural resources and biodiversity. Organic farming workshops, agroecology projects, and community-supported agriculture programs are just a few examples of sustainable agriculture initiatives travelers can get involved in.

Wildlife conservation projects provide yet another avenue for travelers to contribute to environmental protection. By participating in projects that focus on protecting endangered species, conserving habitats, and promoting responsible wildlife tourism, travelers can make a meaningful impact. Whether joining wildlife monitoring expeditions, assisting with wildlife research projects, or volunteering at wildlife rescue centers and sanctuaries, travelers can help ensure the survival of our planet's precious wildlife.

Education and advocacy play a crucial role in environmental conservation, and travelers can use their voice and influence to raise awareness and advocate for conservation efforts. By sharing information about local conservation initiatives, supporting environmental campaigns, and encouraging others to adopt sustainable travel practices, travelers can make a significant difference in their destinations.

Lastly, travelers can offset their carbon emissions by supporting carbon offset projects that fund renewable energy, reforestation, and carbon sequestration initiatives. Many organizations offer carbon offset programs that allow travelers to calculate and offset the carbon footprint of their flights or travel activities by investing in certified carbon offset projects.

By participating in these environmental projects while traveling, travelers can contribute to conservation efforts, promote sustainable tourism practices, and make a positive impact on the environment and local communities. Each action, no matter how small, has the potential to create a ripple effect, inspiring others to join the cause and fostering a collective effort towards a greener future.

It was during my own travels through the rainforests of Costa Rica that I witnessed the transformative power of environmental projects. Knee-deep in mud, surrounded by towering trees and the symphony of wildlife, I joined a group of passionate conservationists on a mission to restore degraded habitats. With each sapling we planted, we felt a sense of hope and renewal. Months later, as the rainy season turned the forest into a lush tapestry of green, we witnessed the fruits of our labor. The saplings we had planted took root and flourished, providing habitat for wildlife and mitigating climate change. But the true measure of our success lay not just in the trees we planted, but in the hearts and minds we touched along the way. Through our actions, we inspired others to join the cause, spreading a ripple of awareness and activism that extended far beyond the borders of the forest.

Environmental projects offer travelers a unique opportunity to make a difference. By getting involved in initiatives that promote conservation, sustainability, and environmental education, travelers can contribute to the protection of our planet's natural wonders. Whether through volunteering, participating in ecotourism activities, or supporting reforestation and conservation efforts, every action counts. Together, we can create a greener and more sustainable world for generations to come.

Sustainability at Sea – Cruises and Alternatives

Chapter 13: Sustainability at Sea – Cruises and Alternatives

The cruise industry, while providing economic benefits and tourism opportunities, also has significant environmental impacts. From air and water pollution to solid waste generation and coastal development, the cruise industry's activities can harm marine ecosystems and coastal communities. It is crucial to address these impacts through sustainable practices and regulatory oversight to minimize harm and ensure responsible tourism.

Fortunately, there are sustainable cruise options and alternative ways to explore the sea that prioritize environmental responsibility. Expedition cruises focus on exploring remote and environmentally sensitive areas, using smaller vessels with eco-friendly features to minimize their environmental footprint. Small-ship cruises offer a more intimate and sustainable alternative to mega-cruise ships, visiting smaller ports and off-the-beaten-path destinations. Sailing expeditions provide a sustainable and eco-friendly way to explore the sea, relying on wind power and renewable energy sources. Ecotourism cruises promote environmental awareness and conservation, partnering with local organizations and indigenous communities. River cruises offer a sustainable alternative to ocean cruises, navigating inland waterways and supporting local economies. Adventure cruises cater to active and adventurous travelers, emphasizing responsible tourism practices. Some cruise companies even offer carbon-neutral options, investing in carbon offset projects to mitigate the environmental impact.

When it comes to responsible and eco-friendly sailing, there are several tips to keep in mind. Choosing a sustainable vessel that is designed and equipped with eco-friendly features is essential. Practicing sustainable sailing techniques, such as sailing with the wind and utilizing renewable energy sources, helps minimize fuel consumption and carbon emissions. Reducing waste and plastic use onboard by bringing reusable items and disposing of waste properly is crucial. Conserving water and energy, supporting sustainable fishing practices, respecting marine wildlife and habitats, and practicing Leave No Trace principles are all important aspects of responsible sailing.

By choosing sustainable cruise options, alternative ways to explore the sea, and practicing responsible and eco-friendly sailing techniques, travelers can enjoy memorable and responsible experiences on the water while minimizing their environmental impact. It is through these conscious choices and actions that we can protect marine ecosystems, support conservation efforts, and ensure a sustainable future for our oceans.

Saving the World – One Selfie at a Time

Chapter 14: Saving the World – One Selfie at a Time

In a world driven by social media, the impact on popular travel destinations cannot be understated. Social media platforms like Instagram, Facebook, and YouTube have revolutionized the way we discover, experience, and share travel destinations. They have influenced traveler behavior, shaped perceptions of destinations, and driven tourism trends. From increased visibility and exposure to destination marketing and promotion, social media has transformed the travel landscape.

One of the key impacts of social media on popular travel destinations is the increased visibility and exposure it provides. Travelers now have a global platform to share their experiences, photos, and videos with a wide audience. This has given rise to the phenomenon of "Instagrammable" destinations, where the visual appeal and photogenic qualities of a location drive its popularity. People are drawn to these destinations for the perfect selfie or the chance to capture a breathtaking view.

Moreover, social media has become a powerful tool for destination marketing and promotion. Travelers, influencers, and destination marketing organizations utilize social media to reach new audiences, showcase unique attractions, and attract tourists to their region. Through targeted advertising, sponsored content, and user-generated campaigns, destinations can effectively market themselves and create a buzz around their offerings.

But the influence of social media goes beyond promotion. It plays a significant role in shaping traveler perceptions and influencing travel decision-making processes. Travelers often turn to social media platforms to research destinations, seek inspiration, and gather recommendations from friends, influencers, and online communities. Positive reviews, captivating images, and personal anecdotes shared on social media can sway travelers' decisions and motivate them to visit specific destinations.

However, the popularity of certain travel destinations on social media has also led to challenges such as overtourism and crowd pressure. Iconic landmarks, natural attractions, and cultural hotspots that have gained popularity through social media hype are now facing the consequences of being overcrowded. The influx of tourists strains local infrastructure, overwhelms natural resources, and disrupts the lives of residents. The need for sustainability and the preservation of local culture and heritage has never been more crucial.

On the flip side, social media trends and viral content can spark new tourism trends and influence traveler preferences and behaviors. From adventure travel challenges to foodie trails and off-the-beaten-path experiences, social media platforms shape travel trends and drive demand for unique and immersive travel experiences that are shareable and Instagram-worthy.

However, the rise of influencers and curated content has sparked debates about authenticity and the role they play in shaping traveler perceptions. While influencers can provide valuable insights and recommendations, concerns have been raised about the authenticity of sponsored content, the influence of curated images on traveler expectations, and the impact of overtourism on local communities and environments.

Despite these challenges, social media has also empowered local communities, residents, and activists to advocate for responsible tourism practices. Online campaigns, petitions, and grassroots movements driven by social media have helped raise awareness about environmental and social issues, and mobilize support for sustainable development initiatives. Social media has become a platform for community engagement and local advocacy, driving positive change and encouraging travelers to make more responsible choices.

Social media has revolutionized the way we discover, experience, and share travel destinations. It has increased visibility, shaped perceptions, and influenced travel decision-making. However, it also presents challenges such as overtourism and the need for responsible tourism practices. Balancing the benefits of social media promotion with the need for sustainability and destination stewardship is essential for the long-term viability and sustainability of popular travel destinations. By promoting responsible sharing and engaging in sustainable travel practices on social media, we can contribute to the preservation of our planet's natural and cultural heritage. Let us save the world, one selfie at a time.

Rediscovering Cities – Urban Oases and Green Getaways

Chapter 15: Rediscovering Cities – Urban Oases and Green Getaways

In the bustling urban landscapes that dominate our world, it is easy to overlook the beauty and serenity that can be found within cities. However, there is a growing movement to transform urban areas into sustainable havens, where nature and modernity coexist in perfect harmony. These urban oases and green getaways offer a respite from the concrete jungle, providing a sanctuary for both humans and the environment.

One such city that stands as a shining example of sustainable urban living is Copenhagen. With its historic landmarks and cutting-edge innovations, this Nordic gem captures the essence of a city that embraces the principles of sustainability and environmental stewardship. As I wandered its charming streets, I was captivated by the seamless blend of old and new, where centuries-old castles stood alongside sleek, energy-efficient buildings.

One of the most striking aspects of Copenhagen's sustainable vision is its commitment to active transportation. The city's extensive network of bike lanes and cycling paths is a testament to its dedication to creating a healthier, more livable urban environment. As I pedaled my way through the city, I marveled at the sight of families, commuters, and tourists alike, all embracing cycling as a way of life. Copenhagen's embrace of bicycles as a primary mode of transportation not only reduces carbon emissions but also fosters a sense of community and well-being.

But Copenhagen's sustainability journey extends far beyond its commitment to active transportation. The city is also a pioneer in green infrastructure, with parks, green spaces, and urban forests seamlessly integrated into its urban fabric. These green oases not only provide a refuge for residents and visitors but also help mitigate the heat island effect, reduce stormwater runoff, and enhance biodiversity. As I explored the vibrant Nørrebro district, I found myself immersed in a world where hip cafes, organic markets, and community gardens coexist harmoniously, showcasing the city's dedication to sustainable living.

Perhaps the most awe-inspiring moment of my journey came when I visited the visionary eco-district of Ørestad. Here, I witnessed the transformative power of sustainable design and green living. Energy-efficient buildings, green roofs, and innovative water management systems seamlessly integrated nature into the urban landscape, creating a thriving ecosystem where people and the environment thrive side by side. Ørestad serves as a testament to the fact that sustainable urban development is not only possible but also essential for creating a brighter future.

Copenhagen's commitment to sustainability goes beyond mere rhetoric; it is ingrained in the city's DNA. It is a way of life, a guiding principle that shapes every aspect of urban planning, design, and daily living. As I bid farewell to this remarkable city, I left with a profound sense of admiration and gratitude for its efforts in building a more sustainable future. Copenhagen serves as a beacon of hope, reminding us that cities can be more than just concrete jungles – they can be havens of sustainability, where nature and modernity intertwine to create a better world for all.

The journey through cities is not just about exploring their vibrant cultures and rich histories. It is also about discovering the hidden gems of sustainability that lie within. From the bike lanes of Copenhagen to the green spaces of Nørrebro, these urban oases and green getaways offer a glimpse into a future where cities and nature coexist harmoniously. By embracing sustainable practices and reimagining urban spaces, we can create cities that are not only livable but also thriving, resilient, and environmentally conscious. So, let us embark on this journey of rediscovering cities, where every street corner holds the promise of a greener, more sustainable future.

The Great Silence – Retreats and Their Green Side

Chapter 16: The Great Silence – Retreats and Their Green Side

———

In the quest for sustainable travel, one cannot overlook the significance of retreats and wellness centers. These havens of tranquility offer a respite from the chaos of everyday life, allowing travelers to unwind, recharge, and connect with nature. But what sets these retreats apart is their commitment to sustainability and environmental stewardship. In this chapter, we will delve into the world of sustainable retreat options and explore the benefits of nature-based relaxation.

Eco-lodges and wilderness retreats are prime examples of sustainable accommodations that prioritize environmental sustainability. These retreats go above and beyond in minimizing their ecological footprint, featuring eco-friendly amenities, renewable energy sources, and organic meals made from locally sourced ingredients. By choosing to stay in these eco-conscious establishments, travelers can immerse themselves in nature while supporting sustainable tourism practices.

Yoga and meditation retreats offer a different kind of sanctuary, one that promotes mindfulness, reduces stress, and cultivates inner peace. Set in natural surroundings such as mountains, forests, and coastal retreat centers, these havens provide guided meditation sessions, yoga classes, and wellness workshops that promote holistic well-being and spiritual growth.

Forest bathing and nature immersion have gained popularity in recent years, with nature-based retreats and wellness programs offering guided experiences that tap into the healing benefits of forest environments.

Through activities such as forest bathing, nature walks, and outdoor exploration, participants can experience relaxation, stress reduction, and mental clarity amidst the beauty of the natural world.

For the adventurous souls, adventure retreats combine outdoor activities such as hiking, kayaking, and wildlife watching with sustainable tourism practices and environmental education. These retreats not only provide opportunities for physical activity and outdoor exploration but also foster environmental awareness and a deeper connection to nature.

Permaculture and sustainable living retreats focus on ecological principles and sustainable practices such as organic farming, renewable energy, and waste reduction. By offering hands-on learning experiences, workshops, and demonstrations, these retreats empower participants to live more sustainably and harmoniously with the natural world.

The benefits of nature-based relaxation are vast and far-reaching. Spending time in nature has been scientifically proven to reduce stress levels, lower blood pressure, and promote relaxation and emotional well-being. Engaging in outdoor activities and nature-based relaxation promotes physical health and fitness, while fostering mental clarity, creativity, and cognitive function. Moreover, nature-based relaxation allows individuals to connect with the natural world, cultivating a deeper appreciation for the environment and a sense of responsibility towards nature conservation. Lastly, it provides opportunities for spiritual growth, personal reflection, and emotional healing, nurturing the soul and fostering a deeper sense of connection to oneself.

When it comes to finding eco-friendly retreats and wellness centers, there are several key factors to consider. Researching sustainable certifications, checking environmental policies, and evaluating facilities and amenities are essential steps in making an informed choice. It is also important to consider the location and surroundings of the retreat, as well as the sustainable practices and initiatives they have in place.

Reading reviews and testimonials from past guests, asking questions, and seeking information directly from the retreat or wellness center can provide valuable insights into their sustainability efforts. Lastly, supporting responsible tourism organizations or eco-friendly travel agencies can help ensure that your retreat aligns with your values and contributes to a more sustainable travel experience.

Personal retreat experiences can be transformative and deeply meaningful. One such experience took place in the serene mountains of Bhutan, a land of breathtaking beauty and spiritual significance. In the village of Paro, I embarked on a journey of self-discovery at a secluded retreat center nestled amidst lush forests and cascading waterfalls. From the moment I arrived, I was enveloped in a sense of peace and serenity that seemed to permeate every corner of the retreat. Each day began with gentle yoga and meditation sessions, followed by hours of exploring the surrounding forests and engaging in group discussions and workshops. The highlight of the retreat was a silent meditation hike to the sacred Tiger's Nest Monastery, where I felt a deep connection to the land and the ancient spiritual traditions of Bhutan. By the end of the retreat, I felt renewed, revitalized, and profoundly grateful for the transformative journey I had embarked upon.

Retreats and wellness centers offer a unique opportunity to reconnect with nature, cultivate inner peace, and promote sustainable travel practices. Whether it be through eco-lodges, yoga retreats, or nature immersion programs, these havens of tranquility provide a sanctuary for the body, mind, and soul. By choosing eco-friendly retreats and supporting responsible tourism organizations, travelers can embark on a journey of self-discovery while leaving a positive impact on the environment. So, let us embrace the great silence of retreats and discover the green side of relaxation.

Footprint-Free Festivals – Can It Be Done?

Chapter 17: Footprint-Free Festivals – Can It Be Done?

As the sun sets on the vibrant landscape of festivals and large events, a dark shadow looms over the environmental impact they leave behind. The revelry and joy of these gatherings often come at a high cost to our planet. The question arises: can we truly have footprint-free festivals?

The environmental impact of festivals and large events cannot be ignored. They generate immense amounts of waste, from single-use plastics to disposable items that end up polluting our land, waterways, and marine environments. The energy consumption required to power these events contributes to greenhouse gas emissions and air pollution. Water usage puts pressure on local resources and ecosystems, leading to scarcity and damage to aquatic habitats. The transportation emissions from attendees traveling to these events further exacerbate air pollution and congestion. Habitat destruction, noise, and light pollution disrupt the natural balance of ecosystems. And let us not forget the social and cultural impacts on local communities, from increased pressure on infrastructure to changes in social dynamics.

However, amidst this bleak picture, there is hope. Sustainable festivals are emerging, paving the way for a greener future. By adopting eco-friendly practices and incorporating environmental considerations into event planning and management, these festivals are striving to minimize their negative impacts and promote responsible stewardship of our natural resources.

Attending sustainable festivals and reducing waste requires conscious effort and environmentally friendly practices. By bringing reusable items such as water bottles, utensils, and food containers, attendees can avoid single-use plastics and disposable products. Proper waste disposal in designated recycling, compost, and trash bins is essential to facilitate recycling and composting efforts. Mindful portion sizes and sharing meals can help reduce food waste. Choosing sustainable transportation options like walking, cycling, or carpooling can minimize carbon emissions. Supporting eco-friendly vendors and offsetting carbon emissions are other ways attendees can contribute to sustainability. Participating in eco-initiatives and spreading awareness about sustainable practices can inspire others to take action. By following these tips, attendees can minimize their environmental footprint and promote a more sustainable festival experience.

One festival that stands out as a beacon of sustainability is the Glastonbury Festival in the United Kingdom. This iconic music festival has long been committed to reducing its carbon footprint and promoting environmental stewardship. With a comprehensive waste management system, including recycling, composting, and waste reduction programs, Glastonbury Festival ensures that recyclable materials are properly processed and diverted from landfills. Renewable energy sources power the festival, minimizing greenhouse gas emissions. Sustainable transportation options are encouraged, reducing traffic congestion and air pollution. The festival also supports environmental conservation and wildlife protection efforts, preserving the natural beauty and biodiversity of its site.

Glastonbury Festival serves as a shining example of how large-scale events can prioritize environmental sustainability. By implementing innovative initiatives and engaging attendees in environmental stewardship, this festival demonstrates that it's possible to enjoy world-class entertainment while minimizing environmental impact and fostering a culture of sustainability.

The journey towards footprint-free festivals is a challenging one, but it is not an impossible dream. With conscious effort, innovative initiatives, and the collective commitment of organizers and attendees, we can create a more sustainable future for festivals and large events. Let us embrace the opportunity to celebrate culture, community, and environmental stewardship hand in hand. The time to act is now.

Traveling Athletic – Experiencing the World with Muscle Power

Chapter 18: Traveling Athletic – Experiencing the World with Muscle Power

In this chapter, we will delve into the world of athletic travel adventures, where individuals explore the wonders of the world under their own steam. Whether it's cycling, hiking, or engaging in other self-propelled activities, these journeys offer a unique and rewarding way to experience nature, culture, and adventure. We will explore the tips and tricks for embarking on these expeditions, as well as share a personal story of an exhilarating athletic travel adventure.

Embarking on an athletic travel adventure requires careful planning and preparation. It is essential to research and plan your route in advance, taking into account factors such as distance, terrain, weather conditions, and points of interest along the way. By using maps, guidebooks, and online resources, you can identify suitable routes and plan your itinerary accordingly.

Packing light is crucial when exploring under your own steam. Only bring the essentials for your journey, including clothing, gear, food, water, and camping equipment. Minimize unnecessary items and opt for lightweight, compact gear that suits your chosen mode of travel.

Safety should always be a priority while exploring under your own steam. Wear appropriate clothing and protective gear, carry essential safety equipment such as first aid kits and navigation tools, and adhere to local regulations and guidelines for outdoor recreation.

Staying hydrated and nourished is vital during these journeys. Carry an adequate supply of water and nutritious snacks or meals to fuel your adventure. Plan your rest stops and meal breaks accordingly to replenish your energy and maintain hydration levels throughout the day.

Respecting nature and wildlife is of utmost importance. Practice Leave No Trace principles and minimize your impact on the environment. Stay on designated trails, avoid disturbing wildlife, and pack out all waste and litter to leave the natural environment pristine for future generations.

Being prepared for emergencies is crucial when embarking on athletic travel adventures. Carry essential safety and survival equipment, such as a mobile phone, emergency whistle, flashlight, and emergency shelter. Familiarize yourself with basic first aid techniques and know how to respond to common outdoor emergencies.

Flexibility and adaptability are key traits to embrace during these journeys. Unexpected challenges or changes in circumstances may arise, and it's important to stay open-minded and adjust your plans or route as needed to ensure a safe and enjoyable experience.

Finally, it's essential to remember to enjoy the journey and savor the moments of beauty, tranquility, and wonder that you encounter along the way. Take time to appreciate the natural landscapes, cultural heritage, and personal connections that make exploring under your own steam such a rich and rewarding experience.

Now, let me share a personal story of an exhilarating athletic travel adventure I embarked on while cycling through the breathtaking landscapes of New Zealand.

THE GREEN ROUTE: DISCOVERING THE WORLD SUSTAINABLY

Several years ago, I found myself drawn to the rugged beauty and pristine wilderness of the South Island of New Zealand. Inspired by tales of epic cycling routes and jaw-dropping scenery, I decided to embark on a solo cycling journey across the island, immersing myself in the natural wonders and outdoor adventures that awaited me.

Setting out from the charming city of Christchurch, I pedaled my way southward, following the winding roads that hugged the rugged coastline and led me through lush forests, rolling farmland, and majestic mountain ranges. Each day brought new challenges and discoveries as I navigated through diverse landscapes and encountered friendly locals along the way.

One of the highlights of my journey was traversing the spectacular Southern Alps, a mountain range that stretches across the length of the South Island and boasts some of the most breathtaking scenery in the world. As I climbed higher into the mountains, I was rewarded with sweeping vistas of snow-capped peaks, shimmering glaciers, and crystal-clear lakes that took my breath away.

Reaching the summit of the iconic Crown Range Road, the highest paved road in New Zealand, was a particularly memorable moment. From this vantage point, I gazed out at the vast expanse of wilderness stretching out before me, feeling a profound sense of awe and gratitude for the opportunity to experience such natural beauty on two wheels.

Throughout my journey, I encountered numerous challenges, from steep climbs and hairpin descents to unpredictable weather and rugged terrain. But with each challenge came a sense of accomplishment and empowerment as I pushed myself beyond my limits and embraced the spirit of adventure that fueled my journey.

As I pedaled through quaint villages, picturesque vineyards, and remote backcountry roads, I forged connections with fellow travelers, shared stories with locals, and immersed myself in the rich culture and hospitality of New Zealand. Every moment was a testament to the transformative power of travel and the joy of exploration.

As I reached the end of my journey in the bustling city of Queenstown, I couldn't help but feel a sense of sadness that my adventure was coming to an end. But as I reflected on the incredible experiences and unforgettable memories I had accumulated along the way, I knew that my journey through the heart of New Zealand would stay with me forever, inspiring me to seek out new adventures and embrace the beauty of the world around me.

Traveling athletic is a remarkable way to experience the world with muscle power. By engaging in activities such as cycling, hiking, and other self-propelled means, individuals can connect with nature, immerse themselves in different cultures, and embark on unforgettable adventures. It is a journey that requires careful planning, preparation, and a spirit of flexibility. Through personal stories and shared experiences, we can inspire others to explore the world under their own steam and create lasting memories while connecting with the beauty of our planet.

The Future of Travel – A Green Horizon

Chapter 19: The Future of Travel – A Green Horizon

The future of travel holds promise for innovative solutions and transformative changes that prioritize environmental conservation, social responsibility, and economic equity. As we envision the possibilities, we find ourselves immersed in a world where sustainable travel takes on new dimensions, pushing the boundaries of imagination and technology.

One speculation takes us into the realm of quantum loop transit systems, where cities and countries are connected through the principles of quantum entanglement. Travel becomes near-instantaneous, but the technology is monopolized by mega-corporations, creating a socio-economic divide. Our protagonists find themselves entangled in a web of corporate espionage and moral dilemmas, navigating the paradoxes of quantum mechanics with light-hearted banter to balance the tension.

In another future, biologically engineered transport becomes a reality. Vehicles are no longer manufactured but grown, adapting to their environment, consuming CO_2, and producing oxygen. However, these living vehicles require a symbiotic relationship with their users, leading to ethical and emotional complexities. The characters' interactions with their quirky, sometimes temperamental vehicles provide comic relief amidst a backdrop of corporate greed and bio-ethical debates.

Advancements in AI bring us to a world of AI-navigated eco-cities. Urban landscapes are transformed into sustainable havens, designed and maintained by advanced AI systems. Personal travel is minimized in favor of efficient public transit systems, but our young hackers find themselves in a cat-and-mouse game with an AI intent on maintaining order. They navigate the city's underbelly, uncovering a conspiracy that threatens the delicate balance between humanity and the machines that serve them.

The physical world ravaged by environmental disasters leads us to virtual reality expeditions. Most travel occurs in vast, immersive virtual reality networks, offering escapism and a platform for exploring concepts of identity and reality. Characters form meaningful relationships and undergo personal growth within the digital frontier, all while questioning the sustainability of retreating into a virtual existence.

A future shaped by climate change takes us to a world of reclaimed ruins and nomadic networks. Communities become nomadic, traveling in sustainable convoys through reclaimed ruins and wild landscapes. These mobile societies practice regenerative agriculture, share a communal ethos, and stand in contrast to dystopian megacities. The story explores themes of belonging and resilience, punctuated by moments of humor derived from the makeshift, often improvised nature of nomadic life.

As we reflect on the potential of sustainable travel, we are filled with optimism and excitement for the transformative impact it can have on individuals, communities, and the planet. Sustainable travel goes beyond mere tourism, becoming a catalyst for positive change. It reconnects us with the natural world, inspiring a deeper appreciation for the Earth's beauty and fragility.

Moreover, sustainable travel empowers local communities and promotes social equity by creating economic opportunities and preserving cultural heritage. It drives innovation and collaboration, inspiring new approaches to transportation, accommodations, and tourism experiences that prioritize sustainability.

THE GREEN ROUTE: DISCOVERING THE WORLD SUSTAINABLY

In our own journeys as sustainable travelers, we recognize the immense power we hold as individuals to make a positive impact. Each decision we make, from choosing eco-friendly accommodations to supporting local artisans, has the potential to create meaningful change. Sustainable travel is not just about minimizing our ecological footprint; it's about embracing a mindset of mindfulness, responsibility, and respect.

As we embark on adventures that enrich our lives and contribute to a more just and sustainable world, we are reminded of the profound impact we can have. The future of travel is a green horizon, where our choices and actions shape a world that future generations can enjoy. Let us embrace this potential and embark on a journey of discovery, connection, and transformation.

The Green Compass – How to Live Sustainably at Home Too

Chapter 20: The Green Compass – How to Live Sustainably at Home Too

Living sustainably goes beyond just being mindful of our actions while traveling. It extends to our everyday lives, where we have the power to make a significant impact on the environment. By adopting sustainable practices at home, we can minimize our carbon footprint, conserve resources, and promote a healthier planet. In this chapter, we will explore some tips and personal anecdotes on how to live a more eco-friendly lifestyle at home.

Reducing energy consumption is a crucial step in living sustainably. By turning off lights, appliances, and electronics when not in use, using energy-efficient LED light bulbs and appliances, and adjusting thermostats, we can significantly reduce our electricity consumption. These small changes not only save us money but also contribute to a more sustainable future.

Conserving water is another essential aspect of sustainable living. Fixing leaks, installing low-flow showerheads and toilets, and collecting rainwater for outdoor use are simple yet effective ways to reduce water waste. Additionally, taking shorter showers and avoiding letting the tap run unnecessarily can make a significant difference in our water usage.

The mantra of "reduce, reuse, recycle" holds true in our everyday lives as well. By minimizing waste through reducing consumption, reusing items, and recycling materials such as paper, plastic, glass, and metal, we can divert waste from landfills and promote recycling. Using reusable shopping bags, water bottles, and containers can also help reduce single-use plastic waste.

Choosing sustainable products is another way to live a more eco-friendly lifestyle. Opting for eco-friendly and sustainably produced products made from renewable materials, organic ingredients, and non-toxic substances can have a positive impact on the environment. Supporting brands and companies that prioritize environmental sustainability, ethical labor practices, and social responsibility can also make a difference.

Our food choices play a significant role in sustainable living. By choosing locally grown, seasonal, and organic foods, we can reduce carbon emissions from transportation and support sustainable agriculture practices. Additionally, reducing meat consumption and incorporating more plant-based meals into our diet can minimize the environmental impact of animal agriculture. Shopping at farmers markets, co-ops, and local farms not only supports small-scale producers but also reduces the carbon footprint of our food.

Practicing sustainable transportation is another essential aspect of living sustainably. Walking, biking, carpooling, or using public transit for daily commutes and errands can significantly reduce our reliance on private vehicles and minimize carbon emissions. Planning trips efficiently, using fuel-efficient vehicles or electric vehicles, and considering car-sharing or ride-sharing options when needed can further contribute to sustainable transportation.

Conserving resources is a fundamental principle of sustainable living. By reducing paper usage, using cloth napkins and towels instead of disposable paper products, and repairing, repurposing, or donating items instead of throwing them away, we can minimize waste and extend the lifespan of our belongings. Educating ourselves and others about environmental issues, sustainability practices, and eco-friendly solutions is also crucial in creating awareness and inspiring positive change.

THE GREEN ROUTE: DISCOVERING THE WORLD SUSTAINABLY

Personal anecdotes can provide valuable insights into the journey of sustainable living. One individual shares their story of embracing a more sustainable lifestyle. They made changes such as reducing energy consumption, adopting sustainable transportation habits, prioritizing locally grown and organic foods, and composting food waste. Through these actions, they not only reduced their environmental footprint but also found a deeper sense of fulfillment and purpose in their daily life.

Living sustainably is an ongoing journey, with new challenges and opportunities always arising. However, by aligning our actions with our values and making conscious choices that prioritize environmental stewardship and social responsibility, we can create a brighter and more sustainable future for generations to come. Each small action adds up to make a meaningful difference in protecting the environment and promoting sustainability in our communities and beyond.

Living sustainably at home is not only possible but also essential for a healthier planet. By adopting sustainable practices such as reducing energy consumption, conserving water, reducing, reusing, and recycling, choosing sustainable products, eating sustainably, practicing sustainable transportation, conserving resources, and educating ourselves and others, we can make a significant impact on the environment. Through personal anecdotes, we can see the transformative power of sustainable living in our own lives. Let us embrace the green compass and embark on a journey towards a more sustainable and equitable world.

Also by Estelle-Maria Reed

Crossroads of Destiny A Journey Through Time and Realms
The Green Route: Discovering the World Sustainably

9 798224 575244